CW00386087

ERRORS AND THE SUSPENSE ACCOUNT

Revision Workbook

Teresa Clarke FMAAT

ERRORS AND THE SUSPENSE ACCOUNT
BY TERESA CLARKE FMAAT

WORKBOOK

Introduction

I have written this workbook to assist students who are studying bookkeeping or accountancy. It is not designed as a teaching tool but more of a revision workbook. I hope it will help you to consolidate your studies so that you can become more confident with this subject and enable you to feel more comfortable with those tricky exam questions.

In accountancy and bookkeeping errors can happen, so we need to know how to correct those errors.

Some errors are shown by the trial balance and use of a suspense account. Other errors are not detected in the trial balance.

Errors that are <u>not</u> revealed in the trial balance are:

<u>Error of omission</u>. For example, a purchase invoice has not been entered into the accounting system at all. Omission means left out.

<u>Reversal of entries</u>. For example, a purchase invoice has been debited to the bank and credited to the purchases account. The credit and debit entries have simply been reversed or put the wrong way around.

<u>Error of original entry</u>. For example, a purchase invoice for £30 was received and was entered as £3 for both the debit and credit entries.

<u>Compensating error</u>. For example, an error in the purchases account on the debit side was £20 too much and an error in the sales account on the

credit side was £20 too much. One error compensates the other or simply matches the other.

Error of commission. For example, a purchase invoice for office supplies has been entered in the motor expenses account in error. They are both the same type of account, i.e., expense accounts.

Error of principle. For example, the purchase of an asset has been entered as an expense in an expense account. These are different types of account.

Errors that are revealed in the trial balance, and therefore create a suspense account are:

Single entry error – one side. For example, a debit entry has been correctly entered, but no credit entry.

Casting error. A ledger account has been incorrectly totalled. Casting means added-up, so this is an adding-up error.

Transposition error. For example, the numbers in one of the ledger balances have been transposed, so £369 has been entered as £396.

Extraction error. For example, when the balance b/d has been taken from the ledger, the wrong number was extracted or taken out of the ledger.

Two debits or two credits. For example, two debit entries have been made instead of a debit and credit entry.

Error of omission. For example, one ledger has been left out, such as the motor expenses.

NOTE: For Level 2 studies you will need to remember the names of these, but for Level 3 studies you will just need to remember how to correct them.

We will also be looking at the suspense account. This is a temporary account that is created for errors in the general ledger. This is essentially the "bucket" that we must empty when correcting the errors. It is commonly used when a bookkeeper does not know where to put something. For example, a business has paid for some insurance, so the bookkeeper enters the credit entry from the bank but does not know what account to put the expense to, so they place it in the suspense account until they can establish where to post it and subsequently correct it. The suspense account can also be used when there is an error in the trial balance, and it does not balance. A suspense account is created to balance the trial balance until the error or errors can be found and corrected.

NOTE: The suspense account can have a debit or credit balance.

Chapter 1 – Correcting errors

Before we can correct an error, we need to identify what error has been made. Once we have found the error, we can decide what should have been done. Then we can work out how to correct the error.

I find it easier to imagine that the error has been made by somebody else and you have been asked to correct it.

Example:
Your colleague, Kim, has entered a purchase invoice for some office supplies which were paid for from the bank like this:

Dr   Motor expenses   £30
Cr   Bank   £30

Step 1: Identify what is wrong with this. The expenses were office supplies, so this is the error. They have been posted to motor expenses in error.

Step 2: Decide what the entries should have been. Ignore what has been done and just write out what *should* have been done.

Dr   Office expenses   £30
Cr   Bank   £30

Step 3: Work out how to correct this. We can see that the bank entry was correct, so we do not do anything with the bank ledger. The motor expenses were debited in error and the debit entry should have been made to the office expenses account. We need to move the expense from the motor expenses to the office expenses.

Let's look at this in T accounts:

Kim made the debit entry into the motor expenses account like this.

Motor expenses

Debit	£	Credit	£
Bank	30		

We need to take this entry out of the motor expenses account and enter it in the office expenses account.

Motor expenses

Debit	£	Credit	£
Bank	30	*Office expenses*	30

Office expenses

Debit	£	Credit	£
Motor expenses	30		

The error has been corrected.

Now we can look at an error that involves the suspense account.

Example:

Ruby has received a payment from a credit customer and has entered it into the accounting records:

Cr   Sales ledger control account   £400

No debit entry has been made.

Step 1: Identify the error. Ruby has correctly made the credit entry but has made no debit entry.

Step 2: What entries should have been made. Remember to write your entries as they *should* have been entered.

Dr   Bank   £400
Cr   SLCA   £400

Step 3: Correct the error. The credit entry that Ruby made was correct, so we do not touch that. The error is with the debit entry which was omitted or left out.

REMEMBER: When we correct entries, we <u>always</u> make both a debit and credit entry.

We can look at this in T accounts. First the entries that Ruby made:

Bank

Debit	£	Credit	£

Sales ledger control account

Debit	£	Credit	£
		Bank	400

To correct this, we need to debit the bank account with the £400, but we must also make a credit entry somewhere. As the credit entry was already correctly made to the SLCA, we use the suspense account.

Bank

Debit	£	Credit	£
Suspense	400		

Suspense

Debit	£	Credit	£
		Bank	400

This can be written as a journal entry:

Dr   Bank   £400
Cr   Suspense £400

This error has been corrected.

You may also come across errors that relate purely to the subsidiary or memorandum ledgers, also known as the sales ledgers and purchase ledgers. These are the ledgers that are not part of the general ledger but relate to individual customers or suppliers. Errors can be made between these. They do not affect the trial balance, but they do need to be corrected.

Before we look at an example, we can remind ourselves of what the subsidiary or memorandum ledgers are. The sales ledger control account gives us a balance of what is owed to us by all our customers, but it does not tell us who owes this money. The sales ledger is a subsidiary ledger which is a record of all the individual accounts. If our business is owed a total of £3,000 from its customers, we can check in the sales ledgers who owes that money.

The sales ledgers are a breakdown of the sales ledger control account. The purchase ledgers are a breakdown of the purchase ledger control account.

The sales ledger control account is part of the double entry system, but the sales ledgers are not.

The purchase ledger control account is part of the double entry system, but the purchase ledgers are not.

Now we will look at an example where we need to correct a subsidiary ledger only:

Magdalena received a payment from a customer, P B Plumbing, for outstanding invoices. She correctly made the entries into the bank and SLCA/receivables accounts. However, in the subsidiary ledger she entered it like this:

Cr   P B Electrical   £500

REMEMBER: The subsidiary ledgers are not part of the general ledger and are not made as double entries. These are merely the break down of the totals in the main ledger.

We can still use the steps to correct this though.

Step 1: Identify the error. Magdalena has entered the payment into the sales ledger of P B Electrical instead of P B Plumbing.

Step 2: What should have been done. The entry should have been made to P B Plumbing.

Step 3: Work out how to correct this. We need to move the entry from P B Electrical to P B Plumbing.

We can see this in the sales ledgers. Firstly, we can see how Magdalena entered this.

Sales Ledger – P B Plumbing

Debit	£	Credit	£

Sales ledger – P B Electrical

Debit	£	Credit	£
		Bank	500

Then we can correct this by debiting the account of P B Electrical and crediting the account of P B Plumbing.

Sales Ledger – P B Plumbing

Debit	£	Credit	£
		P B Electrical	*500*

Sales ledger – P B Electrical

Debit	£	Credit	£
P B Plumbing	500	Bank	500

The error has been corrected.

You have seen that some errors will use the suspense account, and some will not.

If two accounts in the general ledger are affected then no suspense account is needed as we debit one and credit the other, but if the error is only on the debit side or only on the credit side, then we need to use the suspense account.

If the error is only in a subsidiary account, i.e., the sales ledgers or purchase ledgers, then we do not make a double entry, but simply correct the error.

Now we can work through some tasks.

Chapter 2 – Tasks with worked answers

Task 1:

A purchase of goods from R S Holdings for £2,300 has been credited to the purchase ledger of S R Holdings. All other entries were correct.

You are required to correct the error shown in the ledgers below.

Purchase ledger – R S Holdings

Debit	£	Credit	£

Purchase ledger – S R Holdings

Debit	£	Credit	£
		Purchases	2,300

Hint: Use the steps – step 1: identify the error, step 2: decide what should have been entered, step 3: correct the error.

Task 1: worked answer

A purchase of goods from R S Holdings for £2,300 has been credited to the purchase ledger of S R Holdings. All other entries were correct.

You are required to correct the error shown in the ledgers below.

Step 1: Identify the error. The wrong account has been credited with the purchase.
Step 2: Decide what should have been done. The account of R S Holdings should have been credited instead of S R Holdings.
Step 3: Correct the error. We can do this by debiting the account of S R Holdings and crediting the account of R S Holdings.

Purchase ledger – R S Holdings

Debit	£	Credit	£
		S R Holdings	2,300

Purchase ledger – S R Holdings

Debit	£	Credit	£
R S Holdings	2,300	Purchases	2,300

The error has been corrected.

Task 2:

A motor expenses payment has been posted as:

Dr   Rent expenses   £95
Cr   Bank   £95

You have been told that an error was made, and you have been asked to correct this.

Hint: Use the steps.

Step 1: The motor expenses have been posted to rent expenses, but the bank entry is correct.

Step 2: The entries should have been:

Dr   ....   £..........

Cr   ....   £..........

Step 3: Correct the error.

Use the T accounts on the next page to work out what the adjustment needs to be to correct this error, then write it as a journal entry.

Rent expenses

Debit	£	Credit	£

Motor expenses

Debit	£	Credit	£

Journal entry to correct the error:

Dr .... £............

Cr .... £............

Task 2: worked answer

A motor expenses payment has been posted as:

Dr   Rent expenses   £95
Cr   Bank   £95

You have been told that an error was made, and you have been asked to correct this.

Hint: Use the steps.

Step 1: The motor expenses have been posted to rent expenses, but the bank entry is correct.

Step 2: The entries should have been:

Dr   **Motor expenses**   **£95**

Cr   **Bank**   **£95**

Step 3: Correct the error.

Use the T accounts on the next page to work out what the adjustment needs to be to correct this error, then write it as a journal entry.

I will enter the wrong entry, so that I can see what I need to do to correct this.

Rent expenses

Debit	£	Credit	£
Bank	**95**		

Motor expenses

Debit	£	Credit	£

Now I can enter the adjustment needed to correct this, remembering to make one credit entry and one debit entry.

Rent expenses

Debit	£	Credit	£
Bank	95	*Motor expenses*	*95*

Motor expenses

Debit	£	Credit	£
Rent expenses	*95*		

Journal entry to correct the error:

The journal entry is a summary of what I did to correct the error.

Dr   Motor expenses   £95

Cr   Rent expenses   £95

Task 3:

A payment of rent for £125 has been correctly entered into the bank account, but no other entries have been made because the bookkeeper was unsure of how to post this. Instead, he has posted this to the suspense account.

Here is a summary of his entries for this transaction.

Bank

Debit	£	Credit	£
		Suspense	125

Suspense

Debit	£	Credit	£
Bank	125		

a) Make the appropriate adjustments to these accounts to correct the error.
b) Write this as a journal entry.

Dr .... £...............

Cr .... £...............

Task 3: worked answer

A payment of rent for £125 has been correctly entered into the bank account, but no other entries have been made because the bookkeeper was unsure of how to post this. Instead, he has posted this to the suspense account.

Here is a summary of his entries for this transaction.

Bank

Debit	£	Credit	£
		Suspense	125

Suspense

Debit	£	Credit	£
Bank	125		

a) Make the appropriate adjustments to these accounts to correct the error.

We can see that the bank was correctly credited with £125 but the suspense account was used for the debit entry.

We need to move the entry from the suspense account and post this to the correct account.

Bank

Debit	£	Credit	£
		Suspense	125

Suspense

Debit	£	Credit	£
Bank	125	*Rent expenses*	*125*

Rent expense

Debit	£	Credit	£
Suspense	*125*		

The error has been corrected.

b) Write this as a journal entry.

Dr   **Rent expense**   **£125**

Cr   **Credit suspense**   **£125**

Task 4:

Exam questions can include several adjustments in the same task. Don't be alarmed; simply take them one at a time.

A trial balance has been drawn up and a suspense account has been opened with a credit balance of £702.

Several errors have been identified and you have been asked to make the necessary adjustments.

<u>Note</u>: The suspense account should be empty when the correct adjustments have been made.

  a) A payment of £35 made for office supplies has been correctly entered into the bank account, but no other entries have been made.

Dr ....   £ ....

Cr ....   £ ....

  b) A payment of £400 for rent expenses has been entered in the office expenses account. The bank entry was correctly made.

Dr ....   £ ....

Cr ....   £ ....

c) A balance of £1,200 from the motor expenses account has been omitted from the trial balance.

Dr .... £ ....

Cr .... £ ....

d) A cash sale for £92 was correctly entered in the sales account but was entered in the bank account as £29.

Dr .... £ ....

Cr .... £ ....

e) The totals for the following sales have been provided.

Sales	£5,000
VAT	£1,000
Sales ledger control account	£6,000

The bookkeeper has entered these like this:

Dr	Sales ledger control account	£6,000
Dr	VAT	£1,000
Cr	Sales	£5,000

Dr .... £ ....

Cr .... £ ....

Work through this task one error at a time, but before you start, draw up the suspense account. You will need to clear this.

Remember: Not all error adjustments will need the suspense account. Draw up T accounts to help to work out the adjustments needed. Make sure that you make double-entry adjustments for all these errors.

Suspense account

Debit	£	Credit	£

Task 4: worked answer

Exam questions can include several adjustments in the same task. Don't be alarmed; simply take them one at a time.

A trial balance has been drawn up and a suspense account has been opened with a credit balance of £702.

Several errors have been identified and you have been asked to make the necessary adjustments.

Note: The suspense account should be empty when the correct adjustments have been made.

a) A payment of £35 made for office supplies has been correctly entered into the bank account, but no other entries have been made.

The bank entry has been made correctly. This was a payment from the bank, so this was a credit. The debit entry has not been made so we need to debit the office expenses/supplies account. As the credit entry was correct, we use the suspense account for the credit adjustment.

Dr **Office supplies**   £35

Cr **Suspense account**   £35

Enter the suspense account entry in the suspense account ledger now, so that you don't forget to do it.

b) A payment of £400 for rent expenses has been entered in the office expenses account. The bank entry was correctly made.

The bank entry was correct, so we do not touch that. The expense was for rent, but this was entered as office expenses. We need to take it out of the office expenses account and enter it into the rent expenses account. The original entry would have been a debit in the office expenses, so we need to credit that account and then debit the rent expenses account.

Dr **Rent expenses**   £400

Cr **Office expenses**   £400

c) A balance of £1,200 from the motor expenses account has been omitted from the trial balance.

The balance in the motor expenses ledger was omitted from the trial balance, so this was not entered in at all. We need to enter this total in as a debit, as expenses are debits. There is no credit entry to adjust so we use the suspense account for the credit entry.

Dr **Motor expenses**   £1,200

Cr **Suspense account**   £1,200

d) A cash sale for £92 was correctly entered in the sales account but was entered in the bank account as £29.

The cash sale was entered into the sales account correctly, but the wrong amount was entered into the bank account. The bank account entry was made as £29 instead of £92. We need to increase this entry by £63 (£92–£29). The bank entry was a debit as this was money deposited into the bank, so we need to increase the debit was £63. The credit entry was correct, so we need to use the suspense account for the credit entry.

Dr   **Bank**   £63

Cr   **Suspense**   £63

e) The totals for the following sales have been provided.

Sales	£5,000
VAT	£1,000
Sales ledger control account	£6,000

The bookkeeper has entered these like this:

Dr   Sales ledger control account   £6,000
Dr   VAT   £1,000
Cr   Sales   £5,000

We need to think about what should have been done and then compare it to what has been done.

The entries that should have been made were:

Dr	Sales ledger control account	£6,000
Cr	VAT	£1,000
Cr	Sales	£5,000

When we compare what *was* entered and what *should* have been entered, we can see that the SLCA was correct, the sales account was correct, but the VAT account was entered as a credit when it should have been a debit. For this question, it is best to draw the VAT account.

Below is the entry that was made. We need to move this to the credit side. This is a one-sided error, so the debit entry will be the suspense account.

VAT Control account

Debit	£	Credit	£
SLCA	1,000		

In order to move this, we need to enter it twice, or double it.

VAT Control account

Debit	£	Credit	£
SLCA	1,000	**Suspense account**	**2,000**

Cr   **VAT**   **£2,000**

Dr   **Suspense account**   **£2,000**

Suspense account

Debit	£	Credit	£
VAT	**2,000**	**Balance b/d**	**702**
		Office expenses	**35**
		Motor expenses	**1,200**
		Bank	**63**

Then we can balance the suspense account to check that all entries have been made correct and that the account is empty.

Suspense account

Debit	£	Credit	£
VAT	**2,000**	**Balance b/d**	**702**
		Office expenses	**35**
		Motor expenses	**1,200**
		Bank	**63**
	2,000		**2,000**

Task 5:

This is another style of task that could come up in an exam.

The balance on the purchase ledger control account and the balance of the purchase ledgers do not agree or match.

Remember: The purchase ledger control account is the total and the purchase ledgers are the individual accounts of the suppliers. They should match.

The purchase ledger control account has been compared with the purchase ledgers and the following errors have been found.

1. Discounts received of £150 have been entered in the purchase ledger control account but omitted from the purchase ledger.

2. A payment to P Blaseby was debited to the account of K Blaseby.

3. A purchase of £600 has been omitted from the purchases daybook.

4. A contra entry of £300 has been correctly entered in the purchase ledger, but no entry has been made in the purchase ledger control account.

5. A purchase of £300 has been correctly entered in the purchase ledger but has been entered in the purchase ledger control account as £200.

Complete the table below with the adjustments that need to be made to the purchase ledger control account.

HINT: When the word daybook is used in a question it will always relate to the main ledger, e.g., the purchase ledger control account or sales ledger control account.

Work through each of the errors and decide whether they affect the purchase ledger control account or one of the individual purchase ledgers. You will need to find three adjustments.

Adjustment number	Amount £	Debit	Credit

Task 5: worked answer

This is another style of task that could come up in an exam.

The balance on the purchase ledger control account and the balance of the purchase ledgers do not agree or match.

Remember: The purchase ledger control account is the total and the purchase ledgers are the individual accounts of the suppliers. They should match.

The purchase ledger control account has been compared with the purchase ledgers and the following errors have been found.

1. Discounts received of £150 have been entered in the purchase ledger control account but omitted from the purchase ledger.
This error says that the discounts received has been entered in the purchase ledger control account, so that entry is correct. We are only looking for errors that affect the purchase ledger control account so this one can be ignored.

2. A payment to P Blaseby was debited to the account of K Blaseby.
This error describes an error between two purchase ledgers and does not mention any error in the purchase ledger control account, so this one can be ignored.

3. A purchase of £600 has been omitted from the purchases daybook.
This error says that the purchase was omitted from the purchases daybook. Whenever the daybook is mentioned we know that this affects the main ledger, so this one DOES affect the purchase ledger control account. As the purchase was omitted or left out, we can add this

amount to the PLCA. The PLCA balance is a liability and a credit, so this adjustment is also a credit entry.

4. A contra entry of £300 has been correctly entered in the purchase ledger, but no entry has been made in the purchase ledger control account.

This error describes a contra entry as being entered in the purchase ledger but no entry having been made to the purchase ledger control account. As this has been left out of the purchase ledger control account, we need to include this adjustment. A contra entry will ALWAYS reduce the balance, so this will be a debit entry.

5. A purchase of £300 has been correctly entered in the purchase ledger but has been entered in the purchase ledger control account as £200.

This error describes a purchase as having been entered into the purchase ledger correctly, but incorrectly in the purchase ledger control account. The purchase ledger control account needs to be corrected. The entry should have been a credit of £300, but £200 was entered, so we need to add another £100 to the purchase ledger control account.

Complete the table below with the adjustments that need to be made to the <u>purchase ledger control account.</u>

<u>HINT:</u> When the word daybook is used in a question it will always relate to the main ledger, e.g., the purchase ledger control account or sales ledger control account.

Work through each of the errors and decide whether they affect the purchase ledger control account or one of the individual purchase ledgers. You will need to find three adjustments.

Adjustment number	Amount £	Debit	Credit
3	600		√
4	300	√	
5	100		√

Chapter 3 – Tasks

The answers to these tasks are given at the end of the book.

Task 6:

The following adjustments need to be made to the extended trial balance. Write up the journal adjustments required.

REMEMBER: If the error only affects one account, then you will need to use the suspense account for the double entry.

1. Entries need to be made for an irrecoverable debt of £360.

Dr _____ £ _____

Cr _____ £ _____

2. A motor expense of £60 has been entered in the office expenses account.

Dr _____ £ _____

Cr _____ £ _____

3. A rent expense of £600 has been corrected credited in the bank account but entered in the rent expense account as £500.

Dr _____ £ _____

Cr _____ £ _____

4. A bank payment of £200 has been debited to the bank account when it should have been credited.

Dr _____ £ _____

Cr _____ £ _____

Task 7:

The balance on the sales ledger control account and the total of the sales ledgers does not match. The following errors have been identified.

1. A payment received from L Medhurst has been credited to the account of L Mendham.

2. The total of the sales daybook has been undercast by £200.

3. A discount allowed of £50 has been correctly entered in the sales ledger but omitted from the sales ledger control account.

4. A contra entry of £30 has been entered in the sales ledger control account as £300.

5. A payment of £600 has been received from a credit customer when it should have been £700.

6. A credit sale of £650 to T Hills has been credited to the sales ledger control account.

Complete the following table with the 4 adjustments that need to be made to the <u>sales ledger control account</u>.

Adjustment number	Amount £	Debit	Credit

HINT: Work through the adjustments in turn and mark them as _definitely_ affecting the sales ledger control account, _maybe_ or _definitely not_ affecting the sales ledger control account. That way you can work out the ones you know first and then go back and read through the remaining ones again.

Task 8:

The bank statement has been compared to the cashbook and several errors/differences have been found. Complete the table below with the 5 adjustments that need to be made to the cashbook.

Remember: The cashbook is the bank record of the business. It is essentially the <u>bank ledger</u>, so money comes in as a debit and goes out as a credit. The bank statement is the document that the bank produce. When looking through the errors/omissions below you are only looking for those adjustments that need to be made to the business records, the cashbook.

1. Bank interest received of £10 has not been entered in the cashbook.

2. A BACS receipt from a customer of £300 is showing on the bank statement but has not been entered in the cashbook.

3. A cheque for £450 was banked but this had been entered in the cashbook as £405.

4. A direct debit payment for phone expenses of £35 has not been entered in the cashbook.

5. Cheques paid into the bank today totalling £1,200 are not yet showing on the bank statement.

6. A cheque for £99 banked last week was dishonoured by the bank.

Adjustment number	Amount £	Debit	Credit

Task 9:

Short questions:

a) A .... account is a temporary account that can be created to deal with errors or omissions.

b) An error in a subsidiary/individual supplier account *is / is not* part of the double entry system.

c) A sales daybook total that has been overcast by £100 will have an effect on the *sales ledger control account / purchase ledger control account.*

d) A payment of wages for £500 that has been entered into the wages expenses account as £400 and will need to be corrected by which of the following:

Dr	Wages expenses	£100	Cr	Bank	£100
Or					
Dr	Suspense	£100	Cr	Wages expenses	£100
Or					
Dr	Wages expenses	£100	Cr	Suspense	£100

e) A bookkeeper entered a purchase for £30 on the wrong side of the bank account. What is the correct adjustment for this?

Dr Bank   *£30*   *Cr*   *Suspense*   *£30*

Or

Dr Bank   *£60*   *Cr*   *Suspense*   *£60*

Or

Dr Suspense   *£30*   *Cr*   *Bank*   *£30*

Or

Dr Suspense   *£60*   *Cr*   *Bank*   *£60*

f) True or false?

A suspense account will always have a credit balance	*True/False*
A suspense account will always have a debit balance	*True/False*
A suspense account is opened when the trial balance does not balance.	*True/False*
A suspense account must be cleared before the financial statements are drawn up.	*True/False*
Not all errors can be identified in a trial balance	*True/False*

Task 10:

You have been provided with a trial balance from George's Removals. The following errors have been identified and you have been asked to write up the journal entries to correct them.

Hint: Even though the task is asking for your answers as journal entries, it is a good idea to draw up the T accounts or ledgers to help avoid mistakes.

Remember: The suspense account is not needed for all adjustments; only those where only one side needs to be adjusted.

a) A cash sale of £40 has not been entered into the accounting records.

Ledger	Debit £	Credit £

b) A purchase of a new removal van for £3,000 has been entered in the motor expenses account.

Ledger	Debit £	Credit £

c) The sales returns account has been overcast by £30.

Ledger	Debit £	Credit £

d) Discounts received of £25 has been correctly entered in the discounts received account but no other entry has been made.

Ledger	Debit £	Credit £

e) A payment for office expenses of £15 has been debited to both the offices expenses account and the bank account.

Ledger	Debit £	Credit £

Task 11:

The figures from the sales daybook have been correctly totalled below.

Sales ledger control account	£17,844
Sales	£14,870
VAT	£2,974

The bookkeeper has posted these like this:

Cr Sales ledger control account	£17,844
Cr Sales	£14,870
Cr VAT	£2,974

As a result of this error a suspense account has been opened.

You have been asked to correct the error and clear the suspense account.

Hint: Find the error first and leave any correct entries alone. Decide what needs to be done to correct that error.

Suspense account

Debit	£	Credit	£
Balance b/d	35,688		

....

Debit	£	Credit	£

Task 12:

You are working on the accounting records for Dove Enterprises and have been asked to make entries for the following errors and adjustments.

A payment for office expenses of £3,000 has been made from the bank. The correct entry was made in the bank account, but the expenses were posted to office fixtures and fittings.

Ledger	Debit £	Credit £

An entry was made for an irrecoverable debt of £380 in the irrecoverable debts account, but no other entry was made.

Ledger	Debit £	Credit £

No entries have been made for the closing inventory. This was valued at £30,000, but some items which has originally cost £1,200 will be sold for £600 as they are slightly damaged.

Ledger	Debit £	Credit £

A payment for wages of £808 has been correctly entered in the wages expenses account but has been entered in the bank account as £880.

Ledger	Debit £	Credit £

The purchase returns daybook has been overcast by £50.

Ledger	Debit £	Credit £

Discounts received of £30 has been entered correctly in the PLCA but has been entered in the discounts allowed account as a debit.

Note: This is a tricky one so think about it. You will need to remove the incorrect entry before posting the correct entry.

Ledger	Debit £	Credit £

Task 13:

a) A bookkeeper has entered a payment from a customer on the wrong side of the receivables account. What effect will this have on the receivables account?

The receivables account balance will be higher than it should have.

The receivables account balance will be lower than it should have.

b) A trial balance has been drawn up and the credit side totals £236,874 and the debit side totals £234,555. If a suspense account is opened what will be the balance of this?

Dr   £2,319

Or

Cr   £2,319

c) A debit cash balance of £200 is omitted from the trial balance. What effect will this have on the trial balance?

The debit side will be higher than the credit side.

The credit side will be higher than the debit side.

There will be no effect on the trial balance.

d) A payment of office expenses is made from the bank of £25. It is entered in both the office expenses account and the bank account as £52. What effect will this have on the trial balance?

The debit side will be higher than the credit side.

The credit side will be higher than the debit side.

There will be no effect on the trial balance.

e) A purchase of goods from Michael's Stores for £35 has been credited to the purchase ledger as £25. What effect will this have on the trial balance?

The debit side will be higher than the credit side.

The credit side will be higher than the debit side.

There will be no effect on the trial balance.

f) If a cheque payment received is subsequently dishonoured, which accounts need to be adjusted?

Bank and SLCA

Bank and PLCA

SLCA and sales

PLCA and sales

Task 14:

A trial balance has been drawn up and a suspense account opened with a debit balance of £430. The following errors have been found.

You have been asked to make the necessary journal entries to correct the errors and clear the suspense account shown at the bottom of this task.

The petty cash account has been undercast by £30.

Ledger	Debit £	Credit £

Rent expenses of £600 paid from the bank have correctly entered in the bank account but have been debited to the office expenses account.

Ledger	Debit £	Credit £

The sales returns daybook has been overcast by £100.

Ledger	Debit £	Credit £

The VAT control account balance of £200 has been entered into the trial balance as a credit when it should have been a debit.

Ledger	Debit £	Credit £

A payment for insurance of £350 has been entered in both the bank account and the insurance expense account as £530.

Ledger	Debit £	Credit £

Suspense account

Debit	£	Credit	£
Balance b/d			

Task 15:

Identify whether the following errors will affect the balance on the purchase ledger control account.

Error	Will affect the PLCA	Will not affect the PLCA
A payment to a supplier has been entered in the PLCA but no entry has been made in the purchase ledger.		
The purchases daybook has been undercast by £300.		
A payment to J Khan has been entered into the purchase ledger of L Khan.		
A prompt payment discount has been omitted from the purchase ledger control account.		
A contra entry has been entered in the purchase ledger but not in the PLCA.		
A purchase invoice has been entered on the debit side of the purchase ledger control account.		
Payment to a supplier of £500 has been entered in the purchase ledger control account as £400.		

Chapter 4 – Answers

Task 6:

The following adjustments need to be made to the extended trial balance. Write up the journal adjustments required.

REMEMBER: If the error only affects one account, then you will need to use the suspense account for the double entry.

1. Entries need to be made for an irrecoverable debt of £360.
   The irrecoverable debt is an expense to the business, so this is a debit. The sales ledger control account is reduced by this amount, so this is a credit, reducing the asset.

Dr	**Irrecoverable debt**	£	**360**
Cr	**Sales ledger control account**	£	**360**

2. A motor expense of £60 has been entered in the office expenses account.
   The motor expense has been entered into the wrong account, so we need to remove it from the expense account as a credit and then debit this to the correct expense account.

Dr	**Motor expenses**	£	**60**
Cr	**Office expenses**	£	**60**

3. A rent expense of £600 has been corrected credited in the bank account but entered in the rent expense account as £500.

The rent expense was correctly entered in the bank account, so we do not need to adjust the bank account. The rent expense account was only debited with £500, and it should have been £600. We need to increase the rent expense by £100. Because the credit entry was correct, we use the suspense account for the double entry.

Dr	**Rent expenses**	£	100
Cr	**Suspense account**	£	100

4. A bank payment of £200 has been debited to the bank account when it should have been credited.

The bank payment was debited to the bank account instead of being credited. We need to move this payment from the debit side to the credit side. If we enter this once it will cancel out the transaction, so we need to enter it twice to move it. As there is no other account affected here, the double entry is the suspense account.

Dr	**Suspense**	£	400
Cr	**Bank**	£	400

Task 7:

The balance on the sales ledger control account and the total of the sales ledgers does not match. The following errors have been identified.

1. A payment received from L Medhurst has been credited to the account of L Mendham.

This error is with the sales ledgers (individual accounts) so this can be ignored in this task.

2. The total of the sales daybook has been undercast by £200.

This error mentions the daybook. Remember that the daybook means the main ledger, so this one is one of the errors we are looking for to be corrected in the sales ledger control account. It has been undercast, which means *under-added* so we need to increase the sales ledger control account by £200. The SLCA is an asset, so a debit, so this adjustment is a debit.

3. A discount allowed of £50 has been correctly entered in the sales ledger but omitted from the sales ledger control account.

The discounts allowed has been omitted from the sales ledger control account. This means left out, so we need credit the SLCA to reduce the balance of this account.

4. A contra entry of £30 has been entered in the sales ledger control account as £300.

The contra entry has been entered in the sales ledger control account as £300 instead of £30. This means that the SLCA has been reduced

by £300 instead of £30. We need to add back the difference to the balance by debiting it to the account. The difference is £270, so this needs to be added back to the balance owed to the business.

5. A payment of £600 has been received from a credit customer when it should have been £700.

This type of error can be misleading. However, it does not say that any entries were made incorrectly. It merely says that a customer did not pay enough. So this can be ignored as there was no errors of entry.

6. A credit sale of £650 to T Hills has been credited to the sales ledger control account.

This sale was credited to the sales ledger control account when it should have been debited. We need to move this to the other side. In order to do this, we have to move it once to remove the wrong entry and then enter it again to make the correct entry, essentially doubling the amount.

Complete the following table with the 4 adjustments that need to be made to the sales ledger control account.

Adjustment number	Amount £	Debit	Credit
2	200	√	
3	50		√
4	270	√	
6	1,300	√	

Task 8:

The bank statement has been compared to the cashbook and several errors/differences have been found. Complete the table below with the 5 adjustments that need to be made to the cashbook.

Remember: The cashbook is the bank record of the business. The bank statement is the document that the bank produce. When looking through the errors/omissions below you are only looking for those adjustments that need to be made to the business records, the cashbook.

1. Bank interest received of £10 has not been entered in the cashbook.

   Looking for key words in the adjustment we can see that this says *has not been entered in the cashbook.* This is the first adjustment to enter. It is bank interest received and remember that money goes in on the debit side and out on the credit side. So, this is a debit entry.

2. A BACS receipt from a customer of £300 is showing on the bank statement but has not been entered in the cashbook.

   Again, we can see those key words *has not been entered in the cashbook.* This is another one to enter. This is money received from a customer so goes into the cashbook as a debit.

3. A cheque for £450 was banked but this had been entered in the cashbook as £405.

   This is a cheque showing on the bank statement and in the cashbook, but the cashbook entry was incorrect. The cheque was received by the business, so this was a debit, but the amount was not enough. We need to increase this by £45.

4. A direct debit payment for phone expenses of £35 has not been entered in the cashbook.

This is a direct debit payment which came out of the bank account and says that it *has not been entered in the cashbook.* We add this in on the credit side as it is a payment out of the cashbook.

5. Cheques paid into the bank today totalling £1,200 are not yet showing on the bank statement.

These are cheques paid into the bank which are not showing on the bank statement. This does not affect the cashbook as there is no mention of the entry not having been made there. We can ignore this.

1. A cheque for £99 banked last week was dishonoured by the bank.

This is a cheque that was previously banked but has been dishonoured. Dishonoured means that the cheque has "bounced" or been returned because the customer/payee did not have enough money in their account to pay it. It would have been entered in the cashbook as money received, but it has been bounced so we must take the payment back out again. It originally went into the cashbook as a debit so now we take it out as a credit.

Adjustment number	Amount £	Debit	Credit
1	10	√	
2	300	√	
3	45	√	
4	35		√
6	99		√

Task 9:

Short questions:

a) A ***SUSPENSE*** account is a temporary account that can be created to deal with errors or omissions.

b) An error in a subsidiary/individual supplier account *is / **IS NOT*** part of the double entry system.

c) A sales daybook total that has been overcast by £100 will have an effect on the ***SALES LEDGER CONROL ACCOUNT*** / *purchase ledger control account.*

d) A payment of wages for £500 that has been entered into the wages expenses account as £400 and will need to be corrected by which of the following:

Dr	Wages expenses	£100	Cr	Bank	£100

Or

Dr	Suspense	£100	Cr	Wages expenses	£100

Or

Dr	**Wages expenses**	**£100**	**Cr**	**Suspense**	**£100**

e) A bookkeeper entered a purchase for £30 on the wrong side of the bank account. What is the correct adjustment for this?

Dr Bank   £30   Cr   Suspense £30

Or

Dr Bank   £60   Cr   Suspense £60

Or

Dr Suspense   £30   Cr   Bank   £30

Or

<u>Dr Suspense £60   Cr   Bank   £60</u>

Note: Once to eliminate the error and again to enter it correctly (or double it).

f) True or false?

A suspense account will always have a credit balance	True/***False***
A suspense account will always have a debit balance	True/***False***
A suspense account is opened when the trial balance does not balance.	***True***/False
A suspense account must be cleared before the financial statements are drawn up.	***True***/False
Not all errors can be identified in a trial balance	***True***/False

Task 10:

You have been provided with a trial balance from George's Removals. The following errors have been identified and you have been asked to write up the journal entries to correct them.

Remember: The suspense account is not needed for all adjustments; only those where only one side needs to be adjusted.

a) A cash sale of £40 has not been entered into the accounting records.

This has not been entered at all, so we can simply enter it as it should have been made.

Ledger	Debit £	Credit £
Bank	40	
Sales		40

b) A purchase of a new removal van for £3,000 has been entered in the motor expenses account.

This is the purchase of an asset, but it has been entered in the motor expenses account. We need to take it out of the expense account and move to the asset account. Note that your narrative may be slightly different, but if you write something like van or vehicles or asset, that is fine.

Ledger	Debit £	Credit £
Asset – van	3,000	
Motor expenses		3,000

c) The sales returns account has been overcast by £30.

The sales returns have been overcast or over-added. Sales returns are a debit, and this has been overcast, so we need to lower this by crediting the account with £30. There is no debit entry to adjust so we use the suspense account.

Ledger	Debit £	Credit £
Suspense	30	
Sales returns		30

d) Discounts received of £25 has been correctly entered in the discounts received account but no other entry has been made.

The discounts received has been entered correctly. These are discounts that the business has received from the supplier, so these are a form of income. They reduce the amount owed to the supplier. The discounts received account is correct, so the credit entry is correct. The debit entry will be the purchase ledger control account as it is reducing what the business owes. As the credit entry is correct, we will need to use the suspense account again.

Ledger	Debit £	Credit £
PLCA or Payables	25	
Suspense		25

e) A payment for office expenses of £15 has been debited to both the offices expenses account and the bank account.

We need to look at what is wrong with this. Two debit entries have been made instead of a debit and a credit. The office expenses should be a debit so that is correct. The bank entry should have been a credit, so we need to remove the incorrect entry and enter the correct one, essentially doubling the amount. As the debit entry was correct, we use the suspense account for that side of the adjustment.

Ledger	Debit £	Credit £
Suspense	30	
Bank		30

Task 11:

The figures from the sales daybook have been correctly totalled below.

Sales ledger control account	£17,844
Sales	£14,870
VAT	£2,974

The bookkeeper has posted these like this:

Cr Sales ledger control account	£17,844
Cr Sales	£14,870
Cr VAT	£2,974

As a result of this error a suspense account has been opened.

You have been asked to correct the error and clear the suspense account.

We can see what entries should have been made:

Dr SLCA £17,844 to increase what is owed to the business.

Cr Sales £14,870 to increase the sales total.

Cr VAT £2,974 to increase what is payable to HMRC.

We can see that the error is with the SLCA as this has been entered as a credit instead of a debit. Remember that by entering it once, will remove the error, so we add it again to put in the correct entry, therefore doubling the amount as a debit entry. £17,844 to remove the wrong entry and another £17,844 to put in the correct entry; £35,688.

Suspense account

Debit	£	Credit	£
Balance b/d	35,688	*Sales ledger control ac*	*35,688*

Sales ledger control account

Debit	£	Credit	£
Suspense account	*35,688*		

If the question asked for this as a journal entry, it would be:

Dr   SLCA   £35,688

Cr   Suspense £35,688

Task 12:

You are working on the accounting records for Dove Enterprises and have been asked to make entries for the following errors and adjustments.

A payment for office expenses of £3,000 has been made from the bank. The correct entry was made in the bank account, but the expenses were posted to office fixtures and fittings.

The correct entry was made from the bank, so we know that account is not need for the error adjustment. The office expenses were posted to office fixtures and fittings, so we need to take them out of the fixtures and fitting account and into the expenses account. The error would have been made as a debit because the office fixtures and fittings is an asset account. So, we need to credit that account and then debit the correct expense account.

Ledger	Debit £	Credit £
Office expenses	*3,000*	
Office fixtures and fittings		*3,000*

An entry was made for an irrecoverable debt of £380 in the irrecoverable debts account, but no other entry was made.

The correct entry was made into the irrecoverable debt account and this would have been a debit entry because irrecoverable debts are an expense to the business. The credit entry has not been made. An irrecoverable debt reduces the amount of money that is owed to the business (as this has been written off), so we need to reduce the SLCA/receivables. As the debit entry was correct, we use the suspense account for the debit entry.

Ledger	Debit £	Credit £
Suspense account	*380*	
SLCA / Receivables		*380*

No entries have been made for the closing inventory. This was valued at £30,000, but some items which has originally cost £1,200 will be sold for £600 as they are slightly damaged.

No entries have been made here, so we need to enter both the debit and credit entries. The closing inventory value was given as £30,000 but some of this stock has been valued lower. We need to remove that original value of £1,200 and add in the new value (or the difference).

£30,000 – £1,200 + £600 = £29,400

Or

£30,000 – £600 = £29,400

Closing inventory is entered as both a debit and a credit – one entry going to the statement of profit and loss and one going to the statement of financial position.

Ledger	Debit £	Credit £
Closing inventory SFP	*29,400*	
Closing inventory SPL		*29,400*

<u>Hint</u>: To remember which was around this is, try to remember that closing inventory is an asset. Assets are debits. Assets are in the statement of financial position.

A payment for wages of £808 has been correctly entered in the wages expenses account but has been entered in the bank account as £880.

The wages have been correctly entered into the wages expenses account and this would have been a debit as these are expenses, so we do not touch the wages expense account. The error is with the bank account entry which was entered higher than it should have been. We need to work out how much was entered that should not have been and then remove that from the account. As the entry from the bank was £72 too high, we need to lower this by entering a debit entry into the bank account and use the suspense account for the credit entry.

Ledger	Debit £	Credit £
Bank	*£72*	
Suspense		*£72*

The purchase returns daybook has been overcast by £50.

When a daybook is overcast this will affect the main entries posted from this. When we enter purchase returns, we enter these into the purchase returns account and the purchase ledger control account. These are returns so the normal entry for the purchase returns account will be a credit (as it is the opposite to a purchase). This error means that the credit entry in the purchase returns account was £50 too high, so we need to reduce that account, by debiting it and credit the PLCA.

Ledger	Debit £	Credit £
Purchase returns	*50*	
PLCA / Payables		*50*

Discounts received of £30 has been entered correctly in the PLCA but has been entered in the discounts allowed account as a debit.

The entry for this transaction was correct in the PLCA so we will no touch that account. The error here is that the discounts received have been entered as a debit in the discounts allowed account.

This is a tricky one as the correct entry should have been a credit entry in the discounts received. We can't just move it from one to the other as it will be on the wrong side – try and you will see this.

We need to do this correction in two steps, firstly removing the incorrect entry and then entering the correct one.

Incorrect entry: Dr Discounts allowed – we need to remove this first by crediting this account and debiting the suspense account.

Ledger	Debit £	Credit £
Suspense account	*30*	
Discounts allowed		*30*

This has removed the incorrect entry.
Now we can enter the correct entry.

Ledger	Debit £	Credit £
Suspense account	*30*	
Discounts received		*30*

Task 13:

a) A bookkeeper has entered a payment from a customer on the wrong side of the receivables account. What effect will this have on the receivables account?

The receivables account balance will be higher than it should be.

The receivables account balance will be lower than it should be.

This is because the receivables were increased instead of being decreased, showing a higher balance.

b) A trial balance has been drawn up and the credit side totals £236,874 and the debit side totals £234,555. If a suspense account is opened what will be the balance of this?

_Dr   £2,319_

_Or_

_Cr   £2,319_

The suspense account is added to the lower side so that both sides balance.

c) A debit cash balance of £200 is omitted from the trial balance. What effect will this have on the trial balance?

The debit side will be higher than the credit side.

The credit side will be higher than the debit side.

There will be no effect on the trial balance.

This is because a debit balance was left out meaning that the debit side was lower than the credit side.

d) A payment of office expenses is made from the bank of £25. It is entered in both the office expenses account and the bank account as £52. What effect will this have on the trial balance?

The debit side will be higher than the credit side.

The credit side will be higher than the debit side.

There will be no effect on the trial balance.

Even though this is an error it does not affect the trial balance as both the debit and credit entries were the same.

e) A purchase of goods from Michael's Stores for £35 has been credited to the purchase ledger as £25. What effect will this have on the trial balance?

The debit side will be higher than the credit side.

The credit side will be higher than the debit side.

There will be no effect on the trial balance.

Errors in the purchase ledgers or individual accounts are not shown in the trial balance as they are not part of the double entry system. They are memorandum accounts only.

f) If a cheque payment received is subsequently dishonoured, which accounts need to be adjusted?

Bank and SLCA

Bank and PLCA

SLCA and sales

PLCA and sales

When a cheque is dishonoured this means that it bounced. A payment received is not honoured or paid. We need to add this back to the amount owed and take the payment back out of the bank account.

Task 14:

A trial balance has been drawn up and a suspense account opened with a debit balance of £430. The following errors have been found.

You have been asked to make the necessary journal entries to correct the errors and clear the suspense account shown at the bottom of this task.

The petty cash account has been undercast by £30.

The only error mentioned here is the petty cash being undercast. Undercast means under-added. We need to increase the petty cash account, which is an asset. There is no credit entry to correct, so we use the suspense account.

Ledger	Debit £	Credit £
Petty cash	*30*	
Suspense account		*30*

Rent expenses of £600 paid from the bank have correctly entered in the bank account but have been debited to the office expenses account.

The error here is between the rent expenses account and the office expenses account. We need to take it out of the office expenses account and enter in the rent expenses account.

Ledger	Debit £	Credit £
Rent expenses	*600*	
Office expenses		*600*

The sales returns daybook has been overcast by £100.

This error means that the sales returns daybook was overcast by £100 which is £100 too high. As it was an error in the daybook this will affect both the sales returns account and the sales ledger control account. Both the sales returns and the SLCA need adjusting to reflect this. Sales returns are a debit (opposite to sales) so if we are reducing this, then it will be a credit entry.

Ledger	Debit £	Credit £
Sales ledger control account	*100*	
Sales returns		*100*

The VAT control account balance of £200 has been entered into the trial balance as a credit when it should have been a debit.

This entry has been made on the wrong side, so we need to remove the incorrect entry and post the correct entry, thereby doubling the amount. No other account was affected so the suspense account is used for the credit entry.

Ledger	Debit £	Credit £
VAT Control account	400	
Suspense account		400

A payment for insurance of £350 has been entered in both the bank account and the insurance expense account as £530.

This error has been made in both the insurance account and the bank account so both accounts need to be adjusted. Both have been entered as £530 when they should have been £350. Both have been entered £180 too much. We need to reduce each of them. The original entry for the insurance was a debit as this is an expense, so we need to credit that to reduce it.

Ledger	Debit £	Credit £
Bank	*180*	
Insurance		*180*

When the entries are made into the suspense account it is cleared.

Suspense account

Debit	£	Credit	£
Balance b/d	430	Petty cash	30
		VAT Control	400
	430		430

Task 15:

Identify whether the following errors will affect the balance on the purchase ledger control account.

Error	Will affect the PLCA	Will not affect the PLCA
A payment to a supplier has been entered in the PLCA but no entry has been made in the purchase ledger.		*This states that the entry was made in the PLCA.*
The purchases daybook has been undercast by £300.	*The daybook will always affect the main ledger accounts.*	
A payment to J Khan has been entered into the purchase ledger of L Khan.		*This is an error in the individual accounts only*
A prompt payment discount has been omitted from the purchase ledger control account.	*This has been omitted or left out of the PLCA.*	
A contra entry has been entered in the purchase ledger but not in the PLCA.	*This was not entered in the PLCA.*	
A purchase invoice has been entered on the debit side of the purchase ledger control account.	*This was entered on the wrong side of the PLCA.*	
Payment to a supplier of £500 has been entered in the purchase ledger control account as £400.	*This entry was incorrectly made in the PLCA.*	

I hope you have found this workbook useful. If you have any comments you can find me on my Facebook page: Teresa Clarke AAT Tutoring.

Teresa Clarke FMAAT

Printed in Great Britain
by Amazon

44253742R00046